The Universe

The Universe

Written by Francis Davies

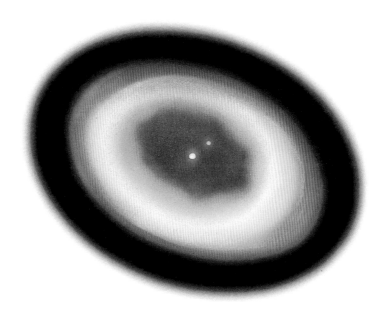

Illustrated by Lorenzo Cecchi

Gareth Stevens Publishing
A WORLD ALMANAC EDUCATION GROUP COMPANY

For a free color catalog describing Gareth Stevens' list of high-quality books and multimedia programs, call 1-800-542-2595 (USA) or 1-800-461-9120 (Canada). Gareth Stevens Publishing's Fax: (414) 332-3567.

Gareth Stevens Publishing would like to thank noted science author Greg Walz-Chojnacki of Milwaukee, Wisconsin, for his kind and professional help with the information in this book. Mr. Walz-Chojnacki is the author of *Celestial Delights: The Best Astronomical Events Through 2001* and *Comet: The Story Behind Halley's Comet.*

Library of Congress Cataloging-in-Publication Data

Davies, Francis.
    The universe / by Francis Davies ; illustrated by Lorenzo Cecchi ; translated
from the Italian by Phil Goddard.
      p. cm. -- (Nature's record-breakers)
    Includes bibliographical references and index.
    Summary: Discusses constellations, stars, comets, meteors, asteroids, moons,
planets, the sun, and more.
    ISBN 0-8368-2476-8 (lib. bdg.)
    1. Astronomy--Juvenile literature. [1. Astronomy.] I. Cecchi, Lorenzo, ill.
II. Title. III. Series
QB46 .D2916   2000
523.1--dc21   99-026883

This edition first published in 2000 by
Gareth Stevens Publishing
A World Almanac Education Group Company
330 West Olive Street, Suite 100
Milwaukee, Wisconsin 53212 USA

Original edition © 1998 by McRae Books Srl. First published in 1998 as *The Universe*, with
the series title *Blockbusters!*, by McRae Books Srl., via de' Rustici 5, Florence, Italy.
This edition © 2000 by Gareth Stevens, Inc. Additional end matter © 2000 by Gareth Stevens, Inc.

Translated from Italian by Phil Goddard, in association with First Edition Translations, Cambridge
Designer: Marco Nardi
Layout: Ornello Fassio and Adriano Nardi
Gareth Stevens editors: Monica Rausch and Amy Bauman
Gareth Stevens designer: Joel Bucaro

Contents

Words that appear in the glossary are printed in **boldface** type the first time they occur in the text.

The Night Sky

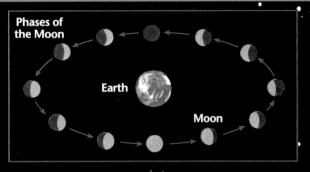

Phases of the Moon

Earth

Moon

The North **Star** is the closest star to the North Pole. This star is sometimes called the polestar.

Milky Way

▲ The Moon is the body closest to Earth. It is Earth's only natural **satellite** and takes about one month to **orbit** our planet. During this time, light from the Sun hits the Moon at different angles. This causes the "phases" of the Moon.

➤ Andromeda is the most distant object the naked eye can see. This galaxy is 2.2 million light-years from Earth. (*For definition of* galaxy, *see page 23.*)

Andromeda

Moon

Venus

Mars

Sirius, the Dog Star, is the brightest star. It can be seen from the Northern Hemisphere in winter months. Sirius is part of the **constellation** Canis Major (*see page 10*). It is about twice as big as the Sun and twenty times as bright.

▼ Venus is the next brightest object in the night sky after the Moon. This planet can be seen clearly at dawn and dusk.

Proxima Centauri is the star closest to Earth. It is 4.3 light-years away and is part of the constellation Centaurus.

Fascinating Fact

Three Egyptian pyramids were built to match the placement of the three stars in Orion's belt. Ancient people may have built them this way for religious purposes.

▼ Auroras can often be seen in places near the North and South poles. Energy from the Sun colliding with gases in Earth's **atmosphere** produce auroras. Auroras take various forms, including changing bands of color that look like curtains blowing in the wind.

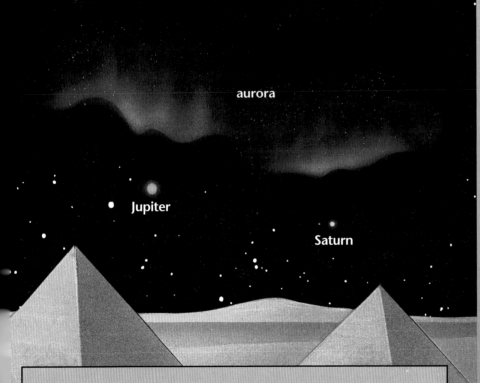

aurora

Jupiter

Saturn

Fascinating Fact

Many ancient monuments were built to line up with objects in the sky. These monuments include Stonehenge, Aztec and Egyptian pyramids, and Chinese and Incan observatories. Some of these monuments face the rising or setting Sun on certain days of the year, while others line up with stars or planets.

Q. WHAT IS A REFRACTING TELESCOPE?

A. A refracting telescope uses two groups of lenses to collect, or gather, light from an object. A telescope has a larger opening than our eyes, so it can collect more light and reveal more details than our eyes alone can.

Q. WHAT IS A REFLECTING TELESCOPE?

A. A reflecting telescope acts just like a refracting telescope, but, instead of lenses, it uses curved mirrors to gather light.

Q. WHAT IS A RADIO TELESCOPE?

A. A radio telescope uses a large dish to gather radio waves emitted by stars and planets. The radio waves have to be strengthened, or amplified, before they can be studied.

Q. WHAT IS A SPACE PROBE?

A. A space probe is a kind of robot that is sent into space. Scientists on Earth control it. A probe sends back information about what it "sees."

Voyager 2 is the most distant human-made object. It was sent into space in 1977 and is now traveling through distant parts of the Solar System.

Venus 4 was the first probe to reach another planet. This probe studied the atmosphere of Venus in 1967.

Voyager 2

sextant

Sailors once used a **sextant** and the stars to navigate the oceans at night.

The Radio Astronomical Telescope of the Academy of Science (RATAN) in Russia is the largest radio telescope. Its dish consists of 900 aluminum panels on a frame 1,890 feet (576 meters) in **diameter**. The Arecibo radio telescope in Puerto Rico is more well-known than RATAN, but it measures only 1,001 feet (305 m) in diameter.

The pillarlike obelisk may be the oldest astronomical tool. The length of its shadow was used to find the height of the Sun in the sky and the angle at which the Sun's rays hit Earth.

Powerful Tools

> The Hubble Space Telescope is the most powerful telescope. Since its launch in 1990, it has gathered much information about some of the most distant areas of the Universe.

Hubble Space Telescope

The Zelenchukskaya Observatory has the largest mirror found in a telescope. Its mirror is 20 feet (6 m) in diameter.

> Galileo was the first person to use a telescope for studying the night sky. His telescope had two lenses mounted in a tube.

Galileo's telescope

The Yerkes telescope, built in 1895, has the largest lens ever used in a telescope. It is 3 feet (1 m) in diameter.

Arecibo radio telescope

Shooting Stars

ORION

Betelgeuse
Heka
Bellâtrix
Alnitak
Mintaka
Sirius
Rigel
Saiph

◄ Orion and Canis Major, or the "dog" following Orion, are the easiest constellations to see. The bright star, Sirius, forms the "eye" of the dog in Canis Major.

Fascinating Facts

Meteoroids are bits of rock or dust orbiting the Sun. Some meteoroids are pieces of **asteroids**. Others are actually pieces of comets left behind as the comets pass near the Sun. When some meteoroids get close to Earth, they go through Earth's atmosphere and burn up in a flash of light. These meteoroids are called meteors, or shooting stars.

Stonehenge

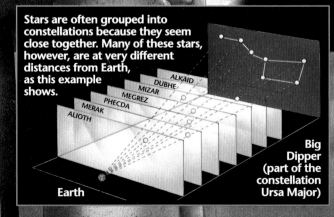

Stars are often grouped into constellations because they seem close together. Many of these stars, however, are at very different distances from Earth, as this example shows.

ALKAID
DUBHE
MIZAR
MEGREZ
PHECDA
MERAK
ALIOTH

Earth

Big Dipper (part of the constellation Ursa Major)

SOUTHERN CROSS

URSA MAJOR

Alkaid
Alioth
Mizar
Dubhe
Megrez
Muscida
Phecda
Merak
Al Kaphra
Talitha
Tania borealis
Tania australis
Alula borealis

▼ The best times for seeing shooting stars are around August 12, October 20, November 16-22, and December 13. These streaks of light in the night sky are pieces of comets or meteoroids that burn up as they enter the atmosphere.

shooting stars

▼ The twelve signs of the Zodiac are the best-known constellations. Astrologers use them to tell the future. Astronomers, however, believe these signs are unique only because the Sun, Moon, and planets move through them.

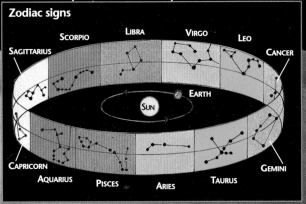

Zodiac signs

SCORPIO · LIBRA · VIRGO · LEO
SAGITTARIUS · CANCER
EARTH
SUN
CAPRICORN · GEMINI
AQUARIUS · PISCES · ARIES · TAURUS

Did you know?

Q. WHAT IS AN ASTROLOGER?

A. In ancient times, an astrologer was a priest who studied the stars. Today, an astrologer is someone who believes that the future can be predicted by studying the positions of the stars and planets in the sky.

Q. WHAT IS AN ASTRONOMER?

A. An astronomer is someone who studies objects outside Earth's atmosphere. Astronomers use observations as well as mathematics and science to study the Universe.

Q. DO CONSTELLATIONS CHANGE?

A. Stars in a constellation are at different distances from the Sun and move separately. This means a constellation's shape may change over many thousands of years.

Q. WHAT IS AN ORBIT?

A. An orbit is the path a body takes as it moves around another body. Also, when a body *orbits* another body, the first body is going around the second body.

11

Comets, Meteorites, and Asteroids

Halley's Comet is the first comet whose return can be predicted by scientists. This comet returns every seventy-five to seventy-six years. In 1986, the *Giotto* probe, a spacecraft sent to study the comet, brought back photographs and information about it.

Ceres is the largest known asteroid and the first asteroid to be discovered. It was first observed in 1801 and is about 621 miles (1,000 km) wide.

Fascinating Facts

• About 65 million years ago, three-quarters of Earth's plant and animal species, including the dinosaurs, suddenly died out. Some scientists believe everything died because Earth was hit by a meteorite. Three large craters on Earth's surface can be traced to this time. The largest crater measures 143 miles (230 kilometers) in diameter.

• In ancient times, some people believed that comets foretold major events, such as earthquakes or military victories.

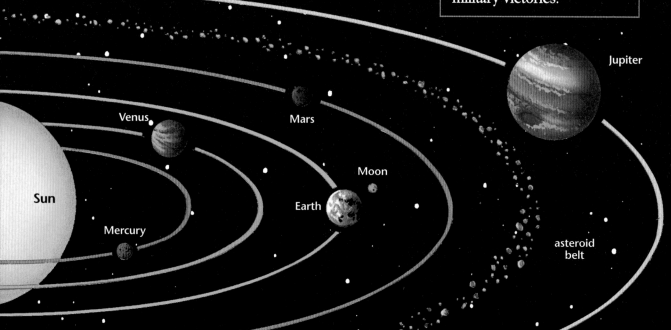

Jupiter

Venus

Mars

Moon

Sun

Earth

Mercury

asteroid belt

The Great Comet of 1843 is the largest comet ever seen. Its tail was 205 million miles (330 million km) long.

comet

gas

nucleus

coma

meteorite

Fascinating Fact

One meteorite weighing over 11,023 tons (10,000 metric tons) hits Earth about every one thousand years. A meteorite weighing 110 tons (100 m tons) hits Earth about every one hundred years. Each year, thousands of tons of meteorites land on Earth's surface, including about one thousand that weigh over 22 pounds (10 kilograms) each. Earth also is hit constantly by space dust.

Possibly the largest meteorite ever to hit Earth landed in South Africa. It made a crater about 217 miles (350 km) in diameter.

Earth

Did you know?

Q. WHAT IS A METEORITE?

A. A meteorite is a piece of rock or metal that reaches Earth without completely burning up in the atmosphere.

Q. WHAT IS A COMET?

A. A comet is a body of ice and rock. When a comet's orbit takes it close to the Sun, it heats up and melts, releasing gases and dust in powerful streams. The gases and dust form a coma, or an atmosphere around its **nucleus**, and a tail millions of miles (km) long. Scientists believe comets originate in an area of the Solar System beyond Pluto.

Q. WHAT ARE ASTEROIDS?

A. Asteroids are small pieces of metal or rock a few miles (km) in diameter. About two thousand asteroids circle the Sun in the asteroid belt between Mars and Jupiter.

The Moon and Other Satellites

Did you know?

Q. WHAT ARE NATURAL AND ARTIFICIAL SATELLITES?

A. Natural satellites are bodies of rock, metal, and ice that orbit a planet. Artificial satellites are objects made by humans and placed in orbit around Earth. We use satellites for scientific study and for communications, usually through the use of televisions and telephones.

Q. WHAT DO WE MEAN BY THE "MAN IN THE MOON"?

A. The Moon sometimes looks like it has a man's face on it. This is caused by the Sun's light reflecting off craters and mountains on the Moon's surface. The Sun's light casts shadows and reflects the different colors of rocks on the Moon, making a "face."

Q. WHAT IS A LUNAR ECLIPSE?

A. A lunar eclipse happens when Earth passes between the Moon and the Sun. The Moon is then in Earth's shadow.

Saturn

Jupiter

Fascinating Facts

• The Moon is about 238,618 miles (384,000 km) away. Its gravitational pull on Earth's oceans causes tides.

• Since the Moon spins on its own axis at the same speed that it orbits Earth, we always see the same side of the Moon.

• Since ancient times, people have used the Moon's steady movement around Earth to measure time.

Ganymede, Jupiter's moon, is the largest satellite in the Solar System. It is 3,270 miles (5,262 km) in diameter.

Saturn's moon, Titan, is the only satellite with an atmosphere. Some scientists believe Titan may have early life-forms on its surface.

Moon

➤ *Apollo 11* astronauts Neil Armstrong and Edwin Aldrin were the first men to walk on the Moon. They stepped onto its surface on July 21, 1969.

Triton

Saturn and Jupiter are the planets in the Solar System with the most moons. Saturn has eighteen moons, and Jupiter has sixteen. Using binoculars, we can see four of Jupiter's moons: Europa, Io, Ganymede, and Callisto.

Charon, Pluto's moon, is the most distant satellite in the Solar System. It was discovered in 1978. Charon is about 746 miles (1,200 km) in diameter, half the size of Pluto (see page 19).

> Io, one of Jupiter's moons, is the most active satellite in the Solar System. Io has active volcanoes that spew gases.

Diameters of Mercury and the largest satellites:	
1 Ganymede	3,270 miles (5,262 km)
2 Titan	3,200 miles (5,150 km)
3 Callisto	2,983 miles (4,800 km)
4 Mercury	3,031 miles (4,878 km)
5 Io	2,256 miles (3,630 km)
6 Earth's Moon	2,160 miles (3,476 km)
7 Europa	1,950 miles (3,138 km)
8 Triton	1,681 miles (2,705 km)

Earth

Earth's Moon is the best-known natural satellite in the Solar System. People have been studying it since ancient times. The Moon is about 4.5 **billion** years old. Like Earth, its surface has mountains, plains, and deep valleys. Unlike Earth, however, the Moon does not have an atmosphere.

15

The Sun

▼ Spicules are the largest "flames" on the Sun. These jets of gas last only a few minutes but can be 497 miles (800 km) across. They can move 19 miles (30 km) a second and reach heights of up to 6,214 miles (10,000 km).

spicules

◄ Sunspots, with temperatures of about 7,232° Fahrenheit (4,000° Celsius), are the coolest parts of the Sun. The rest of the Sun's surface is about 9,932° F (5,500° C). Because sunspots are "cooler," they look darker.

sunspot

➤ Solar prominences are huge, arching flames of gas. A solar prominence can burn as long as a few months. Scientists have noted prominences 93,210 miles (150,000 km) high, 186,420 miles (300,000 km) long, and 24,856 miles (40,000 km) wide. At times, they explode, hurling billions of tons of matter into space.

core

◄ The Sun's core is the hottest part of the Sun. Here, the nuclear reactions that keep the Sun burning take place. Scientists believe the temperature at the Sun's core is about 29 million° F (16 million° C).

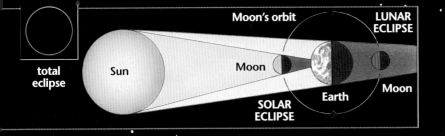

total
eclipse

Moon's orbit

LUNAR
ECLIPSE

Sun

Moon

Earth

Moon

SOLAR
ECLIPSE

▶ The Sun is Earth's main source of energy. Every second, about 200 million billion watts of solar energy reach Earth. That energy is about one hundred thousand times the amount of electricity used on Earth in a year. The Sun produces a total of 386 billion billion megawatts a second.

Fascinating Facts

• Some ancient peoples believed the Sun was a god. During a solar eclipse, many of these people thought a dragon was trying to swallow the Sun. They would hold parades, playing trumpets and banging drums, to frighten the dragon away. A solar eclipse occurs when the Moon passes directly in front of the Sun, blocking its light.

• In the Middle Ages, some people believed sunspots on the Sun were just clouds, like the clouds on Earth. Galileo was the first person to begin a scientific study of the Sun. It is the only star close enough for humans to study its surface in detail.

• The Sun is made almost entirely of hydrogen. The **fusion**, or joining, of hydrogen **atoms** produces energy. The fusion of just .0002 ounces (7 mg) of hydrogen can produce enough energy to meet the needs of a family on Earth, including heat and electricity, for twelve years.

Q. WHAT IS THE SUN?

A. The Sun is a huge ball of gas, about three-quarters of which is hydrogen. Its center is so hot and dense that hydrogen atoms are able to fuse, or join. They then form another chemical element, helium. This fusion of atoms produces energy in the form of heat and light. The Sun has been producing energy for the last 5 billion years.

Q. DOES THE SUN ROTATE?

A. Like all bodies in the Universe, the Sun rotates, or spins, on its own axis. The Sun also moves around the center of the galaxy at about 155 miles (250 km) a second, taking 230 million years to finish an orbit. The Sun is also moving through the Universe along with the rest of the Milky Way galaxy.

solar
prominence

Earth

corona

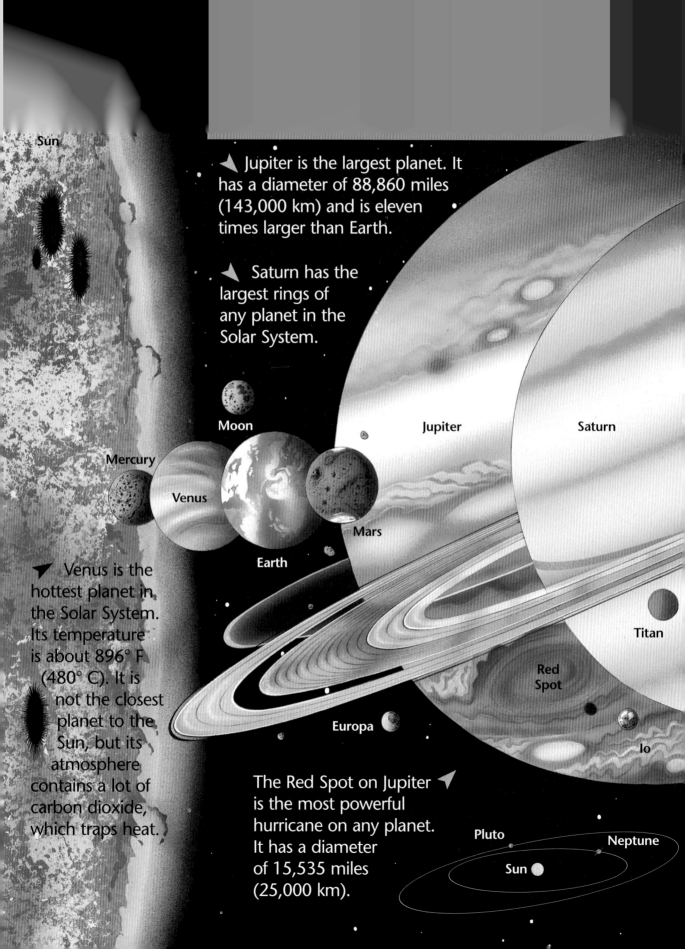

Sun

Jupiter is the largest planet. It has a diameter of 88,860 miles (143,000 km) and is eleven times larger than Earth.

Saturn has the largest rings of any planet in the Solar System.

Moon

Mercury

Venus

Earth

Mars

Jupiter

Saturn

Venus is the hottest planet in the Solar System. Its temperature is about 896° F (480° C). It is not the closest planet to the Sun, but its atmosphere contains a lot of carbon dioxide, which traps heat.

Titan

Red Spot

Europa

Io

The Red Spot on Jupiter is the most powerful hurricane on any planet. It has a diameter of 15,535 miles (25,000 km).

Pluto

Neptune

Sun

▼ Saturn is the least dense planet. It would float if placed in water.

Mount Olympus on Mars is the tallest volcano on any planet. It is 15.5 miles (25 km) high, almost three times the height of Mount Everest.

Uranus

Neptune

Pluto

Charon

▲ Pluto is usually the farthest planet from the Sun, but its orbit sometimes brings it closer to the Sun than Neptune. Pluto is also the smallest planet in the Solar System.

▼ Pluto is the coldest planet. Everything on its surface is frozen solid. Its average temperature is -364° F (-220° C).

Did you know?

Q. WHAT IS A PLANET?

A. A planet is a large body of metals, rocks, and gas that orbits the Sun or another star.

Q. WHY DO THE PLANETS ORBIT THE SUN?

A. The planets orbit the Sun because of the force of **gravity**. Gravity is an attraction that exists between objects. The larger the objects, and the closer the objects, the more the objects are attracted to one another. The larger body — in this case, the Sun — pulls harder than the smaller bodies, such as the planets. Planets do not get pulled into the Sun because they are orbiting it too fast. If Earth slowed down, however, the Sun would pull it in.

Q. WHAT ARE THE RINGS AROUND SOME PLANETS?

A. Rings are pieces of rock and ice orbiting a planet's equator. Saturn, Jupiter, Uranus, and Neptune have rings.

Comets, meteors, and asteroids are the oldest bodies in the Solar System. They are made of material 5 billion years old. Some scientists believe asteroids are pieces of a planet that broke apart.

Comets have the most irre orbits. Some comets come outside the Solar System a then orbit the Sun. Other come into the Solar Syster and then disappear into sp

▲ Mercury has the smallest orbit in the Solar System. It takes only eighty-eight days to orbit the Sun.

co

Sun

Mercury

Earth

comet

Mars

Neptune

Jupiter

Uranus

Venus

Fascinating Fact

Comets form in an area called the Oort Cloud. Sometimes, comets leave this area and travel toward the Sun. Some scientists say that comets are pulled toward the Sun by the gravity of an extinct star, Nemesis. When it was "alive," Nemesis would have been about 2 light-years away from the Sun.

Oort
Cloud

Jupiter

Saturn

Pluto

Pluto and
its moon,
Charon

▶ Pluto is the planet with the largest orbit. Pluto takes 248 years to travel around the Sun.

Q. WHAT IS THE SOLAR SYSTEM?

A. The Solar System consists of the Sun and all the bodies held by its gravity. These bodies include the nine planets, their satellites and rings, over two thousand asteroids, thousands of comets and meteors, and a lot of dust and gas.

Q. HOW OLD IS THE SOLAR SYSTEM?

A. Experts say the Solar System is 4.6 billion years old.

Q. HOW WAS THE SOLAR SYSTEM CREATED?

A. The Solar System formed from a cloud of gas and dust. When the cloud started to shrink from its own gravity, the gas at its center formed the Sun. The rocky planets formed beyond the center. Farther still, the gas planets and icy comets formed.

The Milky Way

Galaxies are the largest objects in space. From above, our own galaxy, the Milky Way, would look like a huge spiral. Our Sun is 30,000 light-years from the galaxy's center. Its light takes nearly 80,000 light-years to reach the other side of the galaxy.

Clouds of dust and gas called nebulae are the darkest objects we can see in the Milky Way. Nebulae block light from stars behind them. They look like dark areas against a bright background.

The galaxy's center is a cluster of stars, nebulae, and other materials. It blocks light from the other side of the galaxy, so we cannot see objects on the far side of the Milky Way.

Sun

Small dwarf galaxies and two large galaxies known as the Large and Small Magellanic Clouds are the closest objects to the Milky Way (*see page 26*).

Stars are the brightest objects in the galaxy. Stars can be dwarfs, giants, or supergiants, depending on their size. They can also be red, brown, yellow, or white in color, depending on their temperature.

Fascinating Fact

The ancient Greeks were the first to call our galaxy the Milky Way. They saw it as a milky white band of stars spread across the night sky. According to Greek myth, this band was milk spilled by Hera, the mother of their gods. The Chinese named the galaxy the Celestial River because its shape reminded them of a river. They thought the stars were fish in this "river." The people of Siberia believed the sky was broken, and objects they saw in the Milky Way were "stitches" used to sew it back together.

THE FORMING OF THE SOLAR SYSTEM — 4.6 BILLION YEARS AGO

1. primordial nebula

2. forming of Sun's nucleus

3. forming of planets

4. thinning of nebula

Did you know?

Q. WHAT IS A GALAXY?
A. A galaxy is a collection of gas, dust, and billions of stars held together by gravity.

Q. WHAT IS A NEBULA?
A. *Nebula* means "cloud" in Latin. A nebula is a huge cloud of dust and gas. Some nebulae are bright, while others are dark.

Q. WHAT IS A GLOBULAR CLUSTER?
A. A globular cluster is a group of stars, ranging from thousands to a million, found in the outer areas of the Milky Way. More stars are in the center of a globular cluster than are on its edges.

Q. OF WHAT IS SPACE MADE?
A. Space is almost empty. On Earth, .06 cubic inch (1 cubic centimeter) of air holds 30,000 million billion **molecules**. In space, the same amount of air holds less than about one atom of hydrogen or a speck of dust.

Did you know?

Q. How does a star form?

A. A star begins as part of a nebula, a cloud of gas and dust. Deep in this cloud, a dense pocket of gas and dust, having a stronger gravitational force than the cloud around it, pulls more gas and dust into itself. The pocket's gravity causes its center to shrink, or contract, and heat up. When this center reaches a temperature of 18 million° F (10 million° C), nuclear reactions begin, and the new star starts to give off energy in the form of light and heat.

Q. Do stars change?

A. All stars eventually expand and turn into **red giants.** Large stars can become supergiants. After becoming a red giant, smaller stars become **white dwarfs** and then cool to black dwarfs, or dead stars. The largest stars explode and scatter material that creates new nebulae. These stars may then become white dwarfs, **pulsars**, or **black holes.**

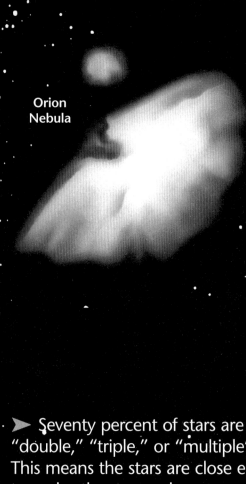

Orion Nebula

➤ M42 in Orion is the most famous nebula we can see with the naked eye. It is dense, with a diameter of about 15 light-years. Scientists think new stars are forming inside it.

➤ Seventy percent of stars are "double," "triple," or "multiple" stars. This means the stars are close enough to each other to revolve around one another. Some double stars can be seen with the naked eye.

supergiant

Sun

◄ The Pleiades are the youngest stars the naked eye can see. The bright cloud around them consists of the remains of the nebula from which they came.

Pleiades star cluster

Nebulae and Stars

Betelgeuse, a red supergiant in the constellation Orion, is the largest star in the night sky. A star can be measured by comparing its diameter to that of the Sun. Betelgeuse is 750 "suns." This means its diameter is 750 times the Sun's diameter. The next largest star is another red supergiant, Antares, in the constellation Scorpio.
It is 640 "suns."

ring-shaped nebula in the constellation Lyra

red giant

supergiant

➤ An exploding star, or supernova, seen in 1054 had the largest explosion in recorded history. This explosion created the Crab Nebula, and the star turned into a pulsar. Gas from the explosion is still moving outward.

Crab Nebula

➤ Black holes are the most mysterious objects in space. When a very large star reaches the end of its life, it explodes. Sometimes, after this explosion, the star becomes a black hole.

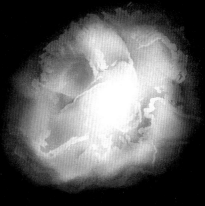

star

black hole

Galaxies

The most distant galaxies seem to be moving away from the Sun. Those farthest away are moving the fastest. Scientists believe this means the Universe is still expanding.

Andromeda

Milky Way

Magellanic Clouds

◀ The force of gravity holds a galaxy together. Each galaxy is part of a larger group that can include hundreds or thousands of galaxies. The Milky Way, for example, is part of the Local Group. This group includes Andromeda and two galaxies known as the Magellanic Clouds.

Groups of galaxies are the largest groups of stars. A group may be spread across a diameter of 10 to 30 million light-years and hold 100 to 300,000 billion stars per galaxy.

Fascinating Fact

Two galaxies collide somewhere in space about every 50 to 100 million years. A collision between two galaxies, however, is not as bad as it sounds. Although a collision happens at a great speed — about 186 miles (300 km) per second — large spaces exist between stars in galaxies. The star closest to the Sun, for example, is 3.2 light-years away. So, two galaxies can collide without the stars in them ever touching. A smaller galaxy, however, may become "stuck" to a larger one because of the differences in their gravities.

two galaxies colliding

Quasars are the most distant objects in the Universe. Quasars are the cores of galaxies about 3 to 18 billion light-years away. Scientists believe quasars have black holes at their centers. These black holes would draw in all sorts of glowing stellar matter, making the quasars appear bright.

GALAXY SHAPES

elliptical   elliptical   spiral   barred spiral

The Universe

Q. How was the Universe created?

A. The most popular theory is that space and matter were created in a huge explosion, called the Big Bang. The Big Bang would have happened 15 to 20 billion years ago.

Q. What happened after the Big Bang?

A. Energy from the explosion created matter. Today, that matter forms the Universe.

Q. Is the Universe still expanding?

A. Yes. Scientists believe the Universe is still growing. Some believe that, although this expansion is slowing down, it will never stop. This is the *open universe* theory. Other scientists believe that gravity will one day stop the Universe from growing. Then the Universe will begin to shrink. This belief is called the *closed universe* theory.

The hottest moment in the history of the Universe, some scientists believe, happened a billionth of a billionth of a billionth of a billionth of a billionth of a second after Big Bang. A tiny ball of high energy was emitted. This ball, containing all the matter that now makes up the Universe, began expanding at great speed. The temperature at this moment was billions of billions of billions of billions of degrees Fahrenheit (Celsius).

The smallest particles were formed as the temperature reached millions of billions of billions of billions of degrees Fahrenheit (Celsius).

Hydrogen atoms were the first atoms. Scientists think they were created when the smallest particles in the Universe joined, or bonded. Hydrogen, a gas, now makes up 97 percent of all matter in the Universe.

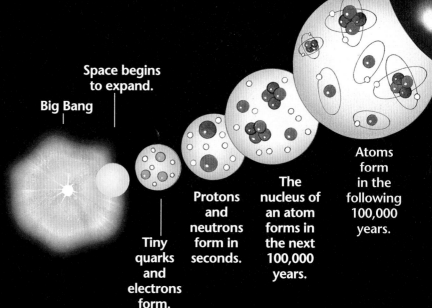

Big Bang

Space begins to expand.

Tiny quarks and electrons form.

Protons and neutrons form in seconds.

The nucleus of an atom forms in the next 100,000 years.

Atoms form in the following 100,000 years.

The Universe is still growing.

The Universe, as it is now, is 15 to 20 billion years old.

The first galaxies form in 1 billion years.

▲ The first star probably formed several billion years after the Big Bang. It would have taken a long time for the Universe to cool enough for the first hydrogen clouds to come together as stars.

Australopithecus

◄ Scientists believe the first humanlike beings appeared about 15 to 20 billion years after the Big Bang.

29

Glossary

asteroids: small planetary bodies made of rock or metal. Thousands of asteroids exist in our Solar System, often orbiting the Sun between Mars and Jupiter.

atmosphere: the gases that surround a planet, star, or moon.

atom: the smallest unit of a chemical element that can exist alone.

billion: the number represented by 1 followed by nine zeros — 1,000,000,000. In the British system, this number is called "a thousand million."

black hole: a burned-out star, with a mass so dense and tightly packed that not even light can escape the force of its gravity.

comet: a body in space that is made of ice, rock, and gas. It has a vapor tail that may be seen when the comet's orbit brings it close to the Sun.

constellation: a grouping of stars in the sky that seems to trace a familiar figure or symbol, after which it is named.

diameter: the length of a straight line through the center of an object; an object's width at its center.

fusion: the joining of atoms. When hydrogen atoms in stars fuse, helium is formed. The energy released during this process is what makes stars shine.

gravity: the force that causes objects like the Sun and its planets to be attracted to one another.

meteoroids: lumps of rock or metal traveling through space. When a

meteoroid enters Earth's atmosphere, it is called a meteor. If it lands on Earth, it is a meteorite.

molecule: the smallest and most basic particle into which a substance can be divided and still be the same substance.

nucleus: the center of an object. In atoms, this center is positively charged and contains smaller particles called neutrons and protons.

orbit: (v) to travel around or revolve around; (n) the path an object takes as it moves around another object.

pulsar: a core of a collapsed star that sends our rapid pulses, or flashes, of light or electrical rays.

red giant: a huge star that develops when hydrogen in the star runs low and the extra heat causes the star to expand.

satellite: a smaller body that orbits a larger body. The Moon is Earth's natural satellite.

sextant: a navigational tool that measures the angular distance between two points, such as a star and the horizon.

star: a glowing cloud of gas that produces its own energy in the form of heat and light.

trillion: the number represented by 1 followed by twelve zeros — 1,000,000,000,000. In the British system, this number is called "a billion."

white dwarf: the small, white-hot body that remains when a star like the Sun collapses.

More Books to Read

Comets, Meteors, and Asteroids.
Seymour Simon (Econo-Clad Books)

Cosmic Light Shows. Eye on the Universe
(series). Bobbie Kalman and April Fast
(Crabtree)

Destination: Jupiter. Seymour Jupiter Simon
(William Morrow & Co. Library)

*Do Stars Have Points? Questions and Answers
About Stars And Planets.* Melvin Berger and
Gilda Berger (Scholastic Reference)

Earth and Universe. Record Breakers (series).
Storm Dunlop (Gareth Stevens)

*Isaac Asimov's New Library of the
Universe* (series). Isaac Asimov, Greg
Walz-Chojnacki, and Francis Reddy
(Gareth Stevens)

*The Planets in Our Solar System. Let's-
Read-And-Find-Out Science Stage 2.*
Franklyn Mansfield Branley
(HarperCollins Juvenile Books)

The Starry Sky. Patrick Moore
(Copper Beech Books)

What is a Shooting Star? Ask Isaac Asimov
(series). Isaac Asimov (Gareth Stevens)

Videos

Astronomy 101. (Tapeworm)

Changing Universe. (Vision Quest Video)

Exploring Space. (WGBH Boston Video)

Great Minds of Science — Astronomy.
(Unapix)

*The Standard Deviants: Astronomy Parts 1
and 2.* (Cerebellum Corporation)

Web Sites

Amazing Space Web-based Activities
amazing-space.stsci.edu/

NASA Kids
kids.msfc.nasa.gov/

The Nine Planets
www.seds.org/nineplanets/nineplanets/

**Starchild: A Learning Center
for Young Astronomers**
starchild.gsfc.nasa.gov/docs/
StarChild/StarChild.html

Welcome to Astronomy for Kids
www.dustbunny.com/afk/

Some web sites stay current longer than others. For further web sites, use your search engines
to locate the following keywords: *astronomy, Big Bang, black holes, comets, constellations,
Hubble Space Telescope, meteors, Moon, planets, satellites, Solar System, stars, Sun,* and *Universe.*

Index